JAN 8 1998

RELIGIONS OF THE WORLD
I Am
Roman Catholic

❋ PHILEMON D. SEVASTIADES ❋

The Rosen Publishing Group's
PowerKids Press™
New York

Published in 1996 by The Rosen Publishing Group, Inc.
29 East 21st Street, New York, NY 10010

First Edition

Book design: Erin McKenna and Kim Sonsky

Photo credits: Cover © Bill Aron; p. 4 © Phyllis Picardi/International Stock; p. 7 © Bob Firth/International Stock; p. 8 © Livio Anticoli/Gamma Liaison; pp. 11, 19 by Philemon D. Sevastiades; p. 12 © P. Hasegawa/Impact Visuals; p. 15 by Olga Palma; p. 16 © Scott Thode/International Stock; p. 20 © Ryan Williams/International Stock.

Sevastiades, Philemon.
    I am Roman Catholic / Philemon Sevastiades.
        p.   cm. — (Religions of the world)
    Includes index.
    Summary: Introduces the basics of Roman Catholicism through the eyes of a Catholic child.
    ISBN 0-8239-2376-2
    1. Catholic Church—Doctrines—Juvenile literature. [1. Catholic Church.] I. Title. II. Series. III. Series: Religions of the world (Rosen Publishing Group)
BX1754.5.S48 1996
282—dc20
                                        96-3288
                                            CIP
                                          AC

Manufactured in the United States of America

Contents

Being Roman Catholic

My name is Victor. I live in Los Angeles. I am a Roman Catholic Christian. Roman Catholics live all over the world in many countries and cultures. We are one religion because we share one faith. We all believe that Jesus Christ is the Son of God.

◀ *Roman Catholic priests often greet members of their churches after Mass.*

Jesus Christ

Jesus Christ is at the center of our faith. As Catholics, we believe that Jesus is the Son of God. We see him as a teacher, as a guide, and as our model. We believe that his life, teachings, and **miracles** (MEER-ah-kulz) are examples for us to follow. My mom says that his life, death, and **resurrection** (rez-ur-EK-shun) changed the world. She says that because of Jesus we can know God in a special way.

Roman Catholics pray to Jesus for guidance. ▶

The Pope

The leader of our Church lives in Rome, Italy. He is called the Pope. "Pope" means "Father." We believe that he has a special relationship with us and with God. We believe that he represents Jesus Christ. He sometimes leaves Rome and visits many places around the world spreading the word of God. I saw him with my family when he came to the United States.

The Pope lives in Rome, Italy, but he visits Roman Catholics all over the world.

The Trinity

When we pray, we often refer to God as the **Trinity** (TRIN-ih-tee). Trinity means "three." We believe that God is three beings: God the Father, God the Son, and God the Holy Spirit. God the Father is the Creator of all things. God the Son was born a human being and lived on earth with us in the person of Jesus Christ. God the Holy Spirit is God's presence in the world, guiding us and teaching us.

This symbol is one way to show the Trinity. ▶
Each circle stands for one part of the Trinity.

Christmas and Easter

At Christmas we celebrate the birth of Jesus Christ. It is my favorite time of year. Christmas is a happy and exciting time. We put a little scene of Jesus' birth underneath our Christmas tree. We go to church at midnight and sing Christmas carols at the Mass.

At Easter we celebrate Jesus' resurrection and his forgiveness of our sins. We prepare for Easter with a time of prayer and **sacrifice** (SAK-rih-fise).

Christmas and Easter are two of our most important holidays.

◀ *We light special candles in church each week before Christmas.*

Baptism

My sister Yolanda was just **baptized** (BAP-tyzd). My mother and father and Yolanda's godparents brought her to church in a special white dress. The priest said some prayers and poured water over her head. Yolanda's godparents promised to help teach her about what Roman Catholics believe and how to live as a Roman Catholic. Now Yolanda is a Roman Catholic too.

A person must be baptized to be part of the Roman Catholic church. ▶

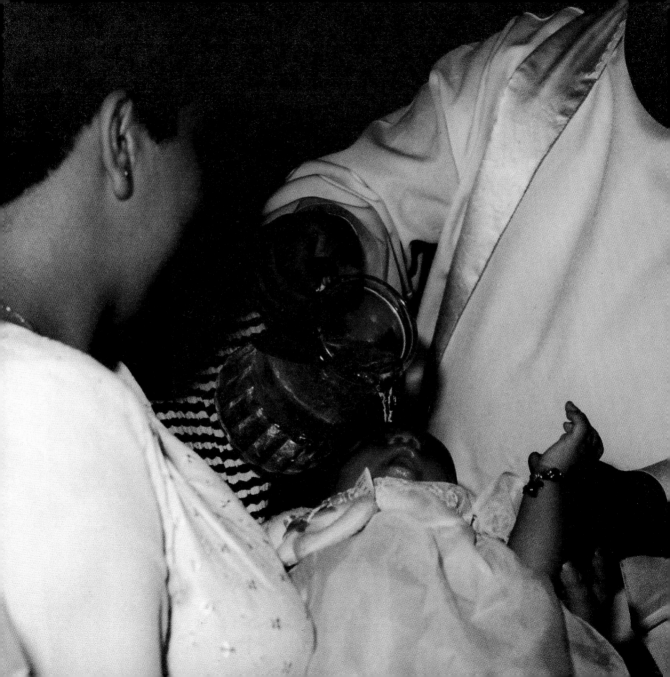

The Mass

On Sundays, and sometimes on other days too, we go to Mass at church. We all sing **hymns** (HIMS), or songs, together. A priest, a teacher of our religion, says the Mass. He reads us a story about Jesus and gives a **homily** (HOM-ih-lee), or sermon, about what Jesus' life means to us. Then we receive **communion** (kom-MYOON-yun). Usually it is a thin wafer of bread that has been blessed. Receiving communion shows that we believe in Jesus Christ and that we are part of the church.

◀ *This boy is an altar server. He helps the priest during Mass.*

Confession and Forgiveness

Sometimes I go to our priest and confess my sins. Sins are things I said or did that were not good. Sins are things that I knew were wrong or things I should have done, but didn't. The priest asks me if I understand why the things I did were wrong. Then he prays for me. He tells me to say a prayer, usually the prayer that Jesus taught. It's called the Lord's Prayer. Then I know I am forgiven.

Many Roman Catholics feel better after confession. ▶

First Communion

When Yolanda is seven, she will receive her first communion. This will be a very special day for her. She will then be old enough to understand and say prayers. When she receives her first communion, she will take part in the entire Mass. Then we will be able to receive communion together.

◀ *Receiving communion is a part of the Mass.*

Confirmation

When I am twelve years old, I will be **confirmed** (con-FERMD). That means that I will become an adult member of the Church. The bishop, who is in charge of many priests in our area, will come to our church. He will bless me and the other people being confirmed. He will pray for the Spirit of God to guide us and teach us how to be good adults.

Glossary

baptism (BAP-tizm) Ceremony that welcomes a person into the Roman Catholic Church.

communion (kom-MYOON-yun) Receiving and eating the blessed bread that Catholics believe is the Body of Christ.

confirmed (con-FERMD) Participating in the ceremony in which children become adult members of the church.

homily (HOM-ih-lee) A lesson on how God wants you to think and behave.

hymns (HIMS) Songs about God.

miracle (MEER-ah-kul) Something wonderful that doesn't normally happen.

resurrection (rez-ur-EK-shun) Miracle of Jesus Christ coming back after his death.

sacrifice (SAK-rih-fys) To give something up.

Trinity (TRIN-ih-tee) The three parts of God.

23

Index